This co

The
SMELLY SOCKS JOKE BOOK

belongs to

_____

The SMELLY SOCKS JOKE BOOK

Susan Abbott

Cover and illustrations by
Mike Roberts

RED FOX

A Red Fox Book

Published by Random House Children's Books
20 Vauxhall Bridge Road, London SW1V 2SA

A division of The Random House Group Limited

London Melbourne Sydney Auckland
Johannesburg and agencies throughout
the world

First published 1988

Set in Century Schoolbook
by JH Graphics Ltd, Reading

Printed and bound in Great Britain by
Cox & Wyman Ltd, Reading, Berkshire

THE RANDOM HOUSE GROUP Limited Reg. No. 954009

Papers used by The Random House Group Limited
are natural, recyclable products made from wood grown in
sustainable forests. The manufacturing processes conform to
the environmental regulations of the country of origin

www.randomhouse.co.uk

ISBN 9781862307902

CONTENTS

B.O. – YUCK!

PITT: What's the most horrible part of the
   human body?
NITT: I'd say the arm, Pitt.

If runners get athlete's foot, what do
   nuclear scientists get?
Missile toe.

STINKER: Our football team has the ultimate deterrent.
PONGO: What's that?
STINKER: Eleven pairs of old boots and twenty-two unwashed socks.

JACQUI: What a strange pair of socks! One is green and smelly and has red spots on it, and the other is blue and smelly and has yellow spots on it!
TACQUI: Yes, and I've got another pair the same at home.

Who wrote *Smelly Socks and Dirty Feet*? *I. Malone.*

Two little girls were paddling on Blackpool beach. Nicky said, 'Coo! Aren't your feet mucky!'

Sticky looked down at her feet. 'They are a bit,' she replied, 'but you see, we didn't come last year.'

The science teacher was talking about space travel. 'Up to now,' he said, 'man has never set foot on Mars.'

'Please, sir,' interrupted Pongo, 'my brother did. He got it squashed all over his shoe.'

Knock, Knock.
Who's there?
Sonia.
Sonia who?
Sonia foot, it's stinking the house out.

What's bright red and very silly?
A blood clot.

What do you call a dirty, frayed, hairy, blood-stained thing found on the bathroom floor?
A used Elastoplast.

What has a bottom at its top?
A leg.

What did Bessie Bunter win when she went on a successful diet?
The No-Belly Prize.

Who wrote *Fat and Exploding*?
Buster Gutt.

What did one ear say to the other?
'I didn't know we lived on the same block.'

Did you hear about Old Blockhead?
He had so much wax in his ears that he became a permanent contributor to Madame Tussaud's.

How do you tell if someone has a glass eye?
When it comes out in conversation.

What did one eye say to the other?
'Between us is something that smells.'

Why didn't Pongo want to have his tooth
out?
*Because he knew parting with it would be
a terrible wrench.*

How did the dentist become a brain
surgeon?
His drill slipped.

DENTIST: Open your mouth wide, Mr
Desmond. You've got an enormous
cavity in your back tooth, you've got an
enormous cavity in your back tooth,
you've . . .
MR DESMOND: All right, you don't have to
keep repeating it.
DENTIST: I didn't repeat it. That was the
echo.

'Your teeth are like the stars,' he said,
As he pressed her hand so white.
He spoke the truth, for like the stars,
Her teeth came out at night.

The flamenco dancer was thrown a red
rose by a beautiful girl in the audience.

After his act was over, she went to ask him what he would do with the rose.

'I'll put it in a glass of water by my bed,' he replied.

'You should put it between your teeth,' reproved the señorita.

'But that's where they'll be,' replied the dancer.

Knock, knock.
Who's there?
Dishwasher.
Dishwasher who?
Dishwasher way I shpoke before I had false teeth.

Did you hear about the man who was arrested while looking at sets of dentures in a shop window?
It was against the law to pick your teeth in public.

Two friends were playing golf. All of a sudden Andy sneezed very violently, and his dentures shot out and broke. 'Don't worry,' said his friend Bandy. 'I'll get you a new set from my brother.'

The next day Bandy brought the new teeth, and Andy tried them. 'They're wonderful! They fit really well!' he exclaimed. 'Your brother must be the most marvellous dentist.'

'Oh, he's not a dentist,' replied Bandy. 'He's an undertaker.'

Did you hear about the farmer who had bad teeth, foul breath and smelly feet?
The doctor said he'd caught foot and mouth disease.

What happened to the man who slept with his head under the pillow?
When he woke up he found the fairies had taken out all his teeth.

Two dentists were discussing a patient. Mr Phang said, 'I wouldn't say his teeth were rotten, but every time he stuck his tongue out one of them snapped off.'

Why is an unhealed wound like a kitten?
They're both a little pussy.

Where would you find a Cockney with
pimples?
'Ackney.

What did the protoplasm say to the
amoeba?
'Don't bacilli.'

Who wrote a treatise on seasickness?
Eva Lott.

It was a rough crossing, and Mrs
Tremblebelly was clinging palely to the
ship's rail. An insensitive steward
marched past. 'Lunch, madame?' he
enquired.
   'Just throw it overboard,' she replied,
'and save me the trouble.'

On the other side of the ship, young
Sidney Greene was also feeling bad.
'Mummy, Mummy, what shall I do?' he
asked weakly.
   'You'll soon find out,' his mother replied.

NICK O'TINE: Do you mind if I smoke?
HONEST JOE: Not if you don't mind if I'm
   sick.

What is a policeman's leg made of?
Truncheon meat.

Knock, knock.
Who's there?
Stan.
Stan who?
Stan back, I'm going to be sick.

Melissa had been given a recorder and a bottle of perfume for her birthday. Her parents had invited some friends round to celebrate, and, as they sat down for tea, Melissa smiled shyly and said to one of her mother's friends, 'If you hear a little noise, and smell a little smell, it's me.'

Why do people emigrate from south-western Ireland?
Because MacGillicuddy's Reeks.

What does the Queen do when she belches?
Issues a royal pardon.

Knock, knock.
Who's there?
Why?
Why who?
Why pa your nose, it's dripping.

The morning bus was very crowded, and a man on his way to work became more and more annoyed by the little boy next to him who kept sniffing loudly.

Eventually he could stand it no longer. 'Haven't you got a handkerchief?' he demanded irritably.

'Yes,' replied the boy, 'but I'm not allowed to lend it to strangers.'

JENNY: I think my brother's built upside-down.
PENNY: How's that?
JENNY: His nose runs and his feet smell.

What does a trade union member do when his nose goes on strike?
Picket.

The glamorous film star was proudly displaying to a group of admirers the new nose she'd just had made by plastic surgery.
  'Have a scar?' asked one.
  'No, thanks,' she cooed. 'I don't smoke.'

Have you heard about the new rock group that performs with a box of paper handkerchiefs?
They're called Electric Catarrh.

'Doctor, doctor, how can I stop my nose from running?'
'Stick out your foot and trip it up.'

What did Mr Vicious do to stop his son biting his nails?
He cut all his fingers off.

MRS SNOOTY: Your little boy's very full of himself, isn't he?

MRS SNOTTY: Yes. I expect it's because he bites his nails.

Why was Lavinia glad when her fingers were chopped off?
Because she didn't have to endure any more piano lessons.

MRS TOE-RAG: Ophelia! Wash your hands before you play the piano!

OPHELIA: But Mum, I only play on the black notes.

CUSTOMER: Your hands are very dirty.

BARBER: I'm sorry, sir, no one's been in for a shampoo yet.

What did the secretary do with old fingernails?
File them.

MRS TAWDRY: Now, Peregrine, have a good wash before you go to your piano lesson.

PEREGRINE: Yes, Mum.

MRS TAWDRY (later): Did you wash your ears?

PEREGRINE: Well, I did the one next to the teacher.

STINKER: Do you look in the mirror to see if you've washed the back of your neck clean?
PONGO: No, I look on the towel.

What's a ringleader?
The first person in the bath.

What do lawyers with malnutrition suffer from?
Red tapeworms.

It was the first time that Prudence had been sunburnt. 'Mum,' she said, 'come quickly. I've got dandruff all over.'

EDIE: I think I've got dandruff.
SEEDY: Will I catch it?
EDIE: Only if you've got nimble fingers.

How do you catch dandruff?
Brush your hair over a paper bag.

What's a good cure for dandruff?
Execution.

What are the little white things in your
   head that bite?
Teeth.

VICKY: Why do you say your little sister is
   like a colander?
STICKY: She leaks.

Do bright eyes indicate curiosity?
No, but black ones do.

SNIFFY: Is your new baby nice and pink?
WHIFFY: No, he's a horrible yeller.

Knock, knock.
Who's there?
Watson.
Watson who?
Watson your head? It looks disgusting.

Knock, knock.
Who's there?
Few.
Few who?
*Phew! There's an awful smell round here,
    is it you?*

Knock, knock.
Who's there?
Colleen.
Colleen who?
Colleen yourself up, you look filthy.

SCURRY OF SKUNKS

Did you hear the joke about the skunk?
Never mind, it stinks!

What did one skunk say to another?
'And so do you!'

What do you get if you cross a skunk with
a boomerang?
A bad smell you can't get rid of.

Mr and Mrs Skunk had two baby skunks
called In and Out. One day In wandered
away, and the two adult skunks and
young Out spent hour after exhausting
hour looking for him. They had almost
given up when Out ran up, panting, 'I've
found him! I've found him!'
  'Well done, Out,' said Mrs Skunk. 'How
did you find him? Was it difficult?'
  'No, quite easy really. I found him by In-
stinct.'

What did the baby skunk long to be when
 he grew up?
A big stinker.

YOUNG SKUNK: Mummy, please may I have
 a chemistry set for Christmas?
MUMMY SKUNK: What, and make the house
 smell!

What do you get if you cross a skunk with
 a porcupine?
A smelly pincushion.

What do you get if you cross a skunk with
 an owl?
A bird that smells but doesn't give a hoot.

What do you get if you cross a skunk with
 a bee?
Something that stinks and stings.

STINKER: Where do fleas go in winter?
PONGO: Search me.

What has fifty legs but cannot walk?
A centipede that's been cut in half.

Who stole the sheets off the bed?
Bed bug-lars.

What do you get if you pour boiling water
   down a rabbit hole?
A hot cross bunny.

What happens if you cross a flea with a
  rabbit?
You get Bugs Bunny.

What do you get if you cross a skunk with
  a bear?
Winnie the Pooh.

What do you get if you cross a skunk with
  a horse?
Whinny the Pooh.

What do you get if you cross a skunk with
  Richard Branson's balloon?
An animal that stinks to high heaven.

What do worms leave round their
  bathtubs?
The scum of the earth.

KEV: My uncle does bird impressions.
TREV: Does he sing?
KEV: No, he eats worms.

What's a polygon?
A dead parrot.

A BIRD IN THE HAND – DOES IT ON YOUR WRIST.

FIRST BIRD: Phew! Look at the speed of that plane!
SECOND BIRD: You'd fly fast if your backside was on fire.

What birds hover over people lost in the desert?
Luncheon vultures.

NIFFY: Our parrot lays square eggs.
WHIFFY: Can it talk?
NIFFY: It can say one word.
WHIFFY: What's that?
NIFFY: Ouch!

What do you get if you cross a chicken with a cement mixer?
A brick layer.

Why don't parents like their children to go near chickens?
Because of their fowl language.

What did Mother Duck say to Father Duck as they rushed to save their

ducklings from being swept over the
weir?
'Quick, quick!'

BESSIE: My cat took first prize in the
    Bigglesworth Cage Bird Show.
JESSIE: Don't be silly! How can a cat take
    a prize in a bird show?
BESSIE: Easily! He ate the champion
    budgerigar.

Little birdie, flying high,
Dropped a message from the sky.
'Gosh,' said Jenny, wiping her eye,
'What a blessing cows can't fly!'

What do you get if you accidentally run
    over a bird while mowing the lawn?
Shredded tweet.

Little Lucy thought it was time her
canary had a bath, as its feathers were
looking a bit grubby. 'I'll put him in the
washing-machine, Mum,' she said,
brightly.
    Her mother was horrified. 'Whatever
you do, don't put him in the washing-
machine. You'll kill him,' she said as she
went out shopping. When she returned,

the poor canary was lying motionless on the draining-board. 'Lucy!' she shouted, 'I told you not to put that bird in the washing-machine!'

'Oh but I didn't, Mum,' said Lucy. 'It was the spin-drier that did it.'

What did the earwig say as he fell off the roof?
' 'Ere we go!'

Three bulls were discussing their future. The first bull said, 'I'm going to be a bull in a china shop.'

The second bull said, 'I'm going to Rome to become a Papal Bull.'

The third bull said, 'I'm going to stay here for heifer and heifer and heifer.'

How do you stop a cockerel crowing at four o'clock in the morning?
Eat him for supper the night before.

BEN: I say, I say, I say, my cockerel's got no knees!
KEN: Take him to London; there are lots of Cockneys there.

Did you hear about the hen who was fed
    on sawdust?
All her chicks had wooden legs.

Why did the chicken cross the road?
For some fowl reason.

What happens to good chickens when they
    die?
They go to oven.

What goes cluck, cluck, cluck, BANG!?
A chicken in a minefield.

A man rushed into a pet shop in a state of
great distress. 'Do you sell penguins?' he
gasped.
    'No,' replied the pet shop owner.
    'Oh dear,' said the man, 'then I've just
run over a nun.'

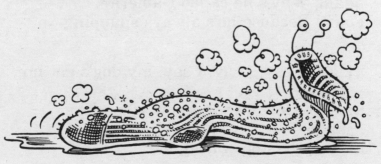

SCOTTY: I say, I say, I say, my dog's got no nose!

SNOTTY: How does he smell?

SCOTTY: Terrible!

What do you call a mongrel in the middle of a muddy lane?

A mutt in a rut.

What did the dog say when he sat on the gravel?

'Ruff!'

CLEAN DEAN: It was kind of you to invite me for tea. But why is your dog sitting watching me and wagging his tail?

DIRTY BERTIE: I expect it's because you're eating out of his bowl.

DORIS: What's your dog called?

BORIS: Camera.

DORIS: Why's he called Camera?

BORIS: Because he's always snapping.

KELLY: I say, I say, I say, my dog's got no tail!

NELLIE: How do you know when he's happy?

KELLY: He stops biting me.

KEV: Every day my dog and I go for a tramp on the common.

TREV: Do you both enjoy it?

KEV: Yes, but I don't think the tramp likes it very much.

31

DORIS: Stinker calls his dog Cigarette.

BORIS: That's a funny name. Why does he call him that?

DORIS: The dog has no legs, so every night Stinker takes him out for a drag.

JONAH: Our dog's just like one of the family.

MONA: Who, your Uncle Herbert?

What did the dog say to the flea?
'Stop bugging me.'

Did you hear about the dog that ate garlic?
His bark was worse than his bite.

Why do bulldogs have flat faces?
Through chasing parked cars.

MRS TENCH: Our dog's bone idle.
MRS STENCH: What makes you think that?
MRS TENCH: Yesterday I was watering the
garden and he wouldn't lift a leg to help
me.

What's the difference between Adolf
Hitler and a dog?
One raises his arm like this (demonstrate
action), *and the other raises his leg like
this* (demonstrate action).

SCOTTY: Why's your dog called Carpenter?
SNOTTY: He does little jobs round the
house.

MRS TAINT: Keep that dog out of the house,
Pongo, it's full of fleas.
PONGO: Keep out of the house, Rover, it's
full of fleas.

What's the difference between a dog with
fleas and a bored visitor?
*One is going to itch, and the other is
itching to go.*

What's the difference between a dog and a flea?
A dog can have fleas, but a flea can't have dogs.

Two fleas came out of the cinema on a wet and windy night. 'Shall we walk home?' asked the first flea.

'No, let's take a dog,' replied the second.

How do fleas travel between London and Manchester?
By itch-hiking.

Mrs Fenella Flea was down in the dumps. 'Whatever's the matter?' asked her neighbour, Mrs Felicity Flea.

'It's the children,' replied Mrs Fenella, 'They're all going to the dogs.'

A fly and a flea in a flue
Were wondering what they should do.
Said the fly, 'Let us flee!'
Said the flea, 'Let us fly!'
So they flew, through a flaw in the flue.

How do you keep flies out of the kitchen?
Put a heap of manure in the living-room.

Two flies met on Robinson Crusoe's head.
One flew away, saying to the other,
'Cheerio, I'll see you on Friday.'

What has four wheels and flies?
A dustcart.

What did the boy maggot say to the girl
    maggot?
*'What's a nice girl like you doing in a joint
    like this?'*

What can fly under water?
A bluebottle in a submarine.

What has antlers and sucks your blood?
A moose-quito.

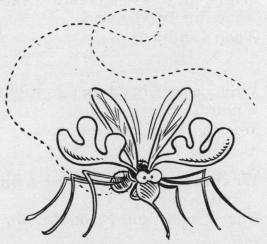

OLD GENTLEMAN: What are you fishing for, sonny?

NAUGHTY NIGEL: I'm not fishing, I'm drowning worms.

What do you call a neurotic octopus?
A crazy, mixed-up squid.

What sits at the bottom of the sea and shivers?
A nervous wreak.

What do you call a baby whale that never stops crying?
A little blubber.

Which kind of sea creature eats its victims two by two?
Noah's shark.

Which creatures didn't go into the Ark in pairs?
Worms: they went in apples.

What happens if you cross a piranha fish with a rose?
I don't know, but I wouldn't try smelling it.

What did one sardine say to the other
    sardine when it saw a submarine?
'There goes a can full of people.'

What swims in the sea, carries a machine
    gun, and makes you an offer you can't
    refuse?
The Codfather.

Which fish terrorizes other fish?
Jack the Kipper.

Why did the lobster blush?
Because the sea weed.

MR REEKING: Have you put the cat out,
    dear?
MRS REEKING: Was he burning again,
    darling?

What do cats like for breakfast?
Mice Krispies.

What do you get if you cross an alley cat
    with a canary?
A peeping tom.

What do you get if you cross a cat with a lemon?
A sourpuss.

What did the cat do after it had swallowed the cheese?
Waited at a mousehole with baited breath.

What do angry rodents send at Christmas?
Cross-mouse cards.

What do you do with a drowning mouse?
Give it mouse-to-mouse resuscitation.

How do you stop a skunk from smelling?
Fix a clothes peg to its nose.

What's the difference between a skunk
    and a mouse?
A skunk uses a cheaper deodorant.

Did you hear about the blind and deaf
skunk whose best friend was a dustbin?

Why did the skunk buy six boxes of paper
    handkerchiefs?
Because he had a stinking cold.

SENSIBLE SANDRA: Where are you going to
    keep your pet skunk?
SILLY SUE: In my bedroom.
SENSIBLE SANDRA: But what about the
    smell?
SILLY SUE: He'll just have to get used to it.

What did the skunk say when the wind
    changed from west to east?
'It's all coming back to me now.'

STAND-UP COMIC: Did you hear the joke
    about the two elephants? They fell over
    a cliff. Boom, boom!

How can you tell when an elephant is in
    the school custard?
When it is more lumpy than usual.

What game did the elephant play with the
ant?
Squash.

How do you tell the sex of elephants?
*Well, first you have to catch them without
their trunks.*

What do you give a seasick elephant?
Lots of room.

What do you get if you walk under a cow?
A pat on the head.

What do you get if you feed a cow on £5
notes?
Rich milk.

What happens to cows in the Antarctic?
They produce ice-cream.

What do you get if you cross a cow with a
camel and an oat field?
Lumpy porridge.

Why did the milkmaid get the sack?
*Because she couldn't tell one end of a cow
from the udder.*

What's the difference between a sick cow
  and a dead bee?
*One's a seedy beast, and one's a bee
  deceased.*

Why do cows lie down in the rain?
To keep each udder warm.

What's the hardest part about milking a
  mouse?
Getting the bucket underneath it.

What do you give a pig with pimples?
  Oinkment.

MR SMELLY: I want a divorce. My wife keeps pigs in the bedroom, and the stench is terrible.

MR STUFFY: But couldn't you open the window?

MR SMELLY: What? And let all my pigeons out?

What do you get if you cross a young goat with a pig?
A dirty kid.

Who wrote *The Bad-Tempered Lion*?
Claudia Armoff.

What happened after the crocodile ate the octopus?
It was armed to the teeth.

What has eight legs, two humps, and flies?
Two dead camels.

Why do giraffes have such long necks?
Because their feet smell.

Knock, knock.
Who's there?

Thumping.
Thumping who?
*Thumping black and hairy with lots of
    legs has just crawled up your trouser
    leg.*

What smells most in the zoo?
Your nose.

What's white and black with red spots?
A zebra with measles.

Why do people keep away from bats?
Because of their bat breath.

What do you get if you cross a dinosaur
    with a wizard?
A Tyrannosaurus hex.

FIRST SNAKE: Are we supposed to be
    poisonous?
SECOND SNAKE: Why?
FIRST SNAKE: Because I just bit my
    tongue.

When an explorer in the jungle saw a
tiger, he fainted. When he came to, he

saw that the tiger was praying, so he said, 'Thank you for not eating me.'

'Shhh,' replied the tiger. 'I'm saying grace.'

What did the lioness say when she found her cubs chasing a man round a tree?
I told you not to play with your food!'

There was a young lady of Riga,
Who went for a ride on a tiger;
They returned from the ride
With the lady inside,
And a smile on the face of the tiger.

What happened when the man put his head in the tiger's mouth to count how many teeth it had?
The tiger closed its mouth to see how many heads the man had.

CIRCUS RINGMASTER: What was the name of that chap who used to put his arm in the lion's mouth?
TRAPEZE ARTISTE: I can't remember, but they call him Lefty now.

What did the River Congo say when a family of hippos sat down in it?
'Well, I'll be dammed!'

NEWSFLASH: An elephant has just been caught doing a ton on the M1. Motorists are advised to slow down and treat it as a roundabout.

Two elephants were arrested at Brighton last summer.
They went swimming and couldn't keep their trunks up.

How many pigs do you need to make a farm really smelly?
A phew.

Why didn't the piglets listen to their father?
Because he was such an old boar.

What do you get if you cross a pig with a halibut?
Dirty and wet.

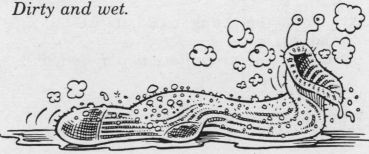

MOTHER: Clarissa! Stop slurping your soup like a pig! Do you know what a pig is?
CLARISSA: Yes, Mother. A pig is a hog's child.

Why was the goat's offspring such a mixed-up kid?
Because he fell in a cement mixer.

A goat was nosing round a rubbish dump when it found a reel of film. It sniffed at it, and then quickly gobbled it up.
Another goat came along. 'Was the film any good?' he asked.
'It was OK,' replied the first goat, 'but I preferred the book.'

What do you get if you cross a sheep with a kangaroo?
A woolly jumper with a pocket.

Why do mother kangaroos hate wet weather?
Because the children have to play indoors.

What do you do with a wombat?
Play wom, of course.

HOUSE OF HORRORS!

What did the monster do to stop his son
  biting his nails?
Cut his toes off.

What do monsters have at 11 a.m. every
  day?
A coffin break.

Why did the cannibal have a bad
  stomach?
*Because he ate people who disagreed with
  him.*

What happens if you upset a cannibal?
You get into hot water.

FATHER CANNIBAL TO DAUGHTER: It's time
  you got married. We'll start looking for
  an edible bachelor.

How do ghosts get through locked doors?
With skeleton keys.

Where do ghosts like to go on holiday?
Goole.

What does a headless horseman ride?
A nightmare.

What is a ghost's favourite pudding?
Apple pie and scream.

Why do demons and ghouls get on so well
  together?
Because demons are a ghoul's best friend.

Why did the mummy leave his tomb after
  3000 years?
*Because he thought he was old enough to
  leave home.*

How did the skeleton know it was going
    to rain?
He could feel it in his bones.

What do you call a skeleton that won't get
    up in the morning?
Lazy bones.

What did the werewolf write on his
    Christmas cards?
'Best vicious of the season.'

What happened when the werewolf fell in
    the washing-machine?
It became a wash and werewolf.

MUMMY MONSTER: What are you doing with
    that saw? And where's your little
    brother?
MATILDA MONSTER: Tee hee, he's my half-
brother now!

MUMMY MONSTER: And did you catch
    everyone's eyes in that dress, dear?
MILLICENT MONSTER: Yes, Mum. I've
    brought them all home for Mervyn to
    play marbles with.

What kind of monster can sit on the end
of your finger?
A bogeyman.

What does a witch who is a poor traveller
get?
Broom sick.

FIRST GHOUL: You don't look too good. Are
you feeling okay?
SECOND GHOUL: No, I'm dead on my feet.

Why didn't the skeleton go to the disco?
Because he had no body to dance with.

What's the definition of a skeleton?
Bones with people scraped off.

What happened when the skeletons rode
  pogo sticks?
They had a rattling good time.

Who was the skeleton who wore a kilt?
Boney Prince Charlie.

What's the difference between a dead dog
  and a musician?
One composes and the other decomposes.

Why did Frankenstein go to see a
  psychiatrist?
Because he thought everybody loved him.

What did the monster family enjoy
  watching on television?
Horror-Nation Street.

How did the glamorous ghoul earn her
  living?
She was a cover ghoul.

What's a ghost's favourite breakfast cereal?
Dreaded wheat.

Where does Sitting Bull's ghost live?
In a creepy teepee.

Where do ghost comedians get their jokes from?
Crypt writers.

What's a vampire's favourite song?
'Fangs for the Memory'.

What's a vampire's favourite sport?
Batminton.

What's a ghost's favourite supper?
Ghoulash.

What trees do ghouls like best?
Ceme-trees.

What do vampires cross the Channel in?
Blood vessels.

What are little ghosts dressed in when it
 rains?
Boo-ts and ghoul-oshes.

Why are ghosts bad at telling lies?
Because you can see right through them.

What's the definition of a cannibal?
*Someone who goes into a restaurant and
 orders the waiter.*

What do guests do at a cannibal wedding?
They toast the bride and groom.

FIRST CANNIBAL WIFE: I don't know what to
 make of my husband nowadays.
SECOND CANNIBAL WIFE: How about a
 curry?

What did the vegetarian cannibal eat?
Swedes.

Why were the Egyptian children worried
 and confused?
Because their daddy was a mummy.

How do you join Dracula's fan club?
Send him your name, address and blood group.

How did the boy and girl vampire fall in love?
At first fright.

What happened when Dracula's girlfriend wouldn't marry him?
He loved in vein.

Where did Dracula keep his savings?
In the blood bank.

What kind of girl does a mummy take on a date?
Any old girl he can dig up.

Where do mummies go if they want to swim?
The Dead Sea.

Why was the mummy a coward?
Because it had no guts.

Why did the two cyclops fight?
*They could never see eye to eye over
anything.*

What keeps ghosts cheerful?
*The knowledge that every shroud has a
silver lining.*

BARBER SHAVING VAMPIRE: Oops! Sorry, sir,
I just cut your chin.
VAMPIRE: That's all right, it isn't my blood.

Which page of a magazine does a vampire turn to first?
The horror-scopes.

What happened to the two mad vampires?
They both went a little batty.

What do vampires eat for breakfast?
Ready Nek.

Why was the young vampire a failure?
Because he fainted at the sight of blood.

After corresponding for some weeks, two members of a lonely hearts pen-pals club decided to meet. The man realized he had better be honest, so he wrote to his lady friend: 'I have to tell you that I am only four feet tall. I have a hunch back, a wooden leg, a glass eye, a broken nose, long greasy hair, and I am covered in acne. If you still want to meet me then I'll be under the clock at Euston Station next Wednesday at 7.30 p.m.'

The lady replied: 'Your friendship is very important to me, and I'd love to meet you next Wednesday. But please will you wear a red carnation and carry a rolled-up copy of *The Times* so that I can recognize you?'

What do ghosts in hospital talk about?
Their apparitions.

How did the ghost song-and-dance act
    make a living?
By appearing in television spooktaculars.

MALCOLM MONSTER: The pretty blonde over
    there just rolled her eyes at me.
MERVIN MONSTER: Well you'd better roll
    them back, she might need them.

MOTHER MONSTER: Millicent! How often
    must I tell you not to eat with your
    fingers! Use a shovel like I do.

Which is a monster's favourite ballet?
Swamp Lake.

What do you call a ghost's mother and
    father?
Transparents.

What do you do with a blue monster?
Try to cheer it up.

Did you hear about the monster who lived
   on little bits of metal?
It was his staple diet.

What kind of cocktails do monsters enjoy?
'Ighballs (eyeballs).

What's a skeleton's favourite drink?
Milk. It's so good for the bones.

What was the cannibal called who ate his
   father's sister?
An aunt-eater.

Why did the monster go to hospital?
To have his ghoul stones removed.

Knock, knock.
Who's there?
Ida.
Ida who?
Ida face, please, it's so ugly.

What can a monster do that you can't do?
Count up to twenty-five on its fingers.

CUTHBERT CANNIBAL: Mummy, I don't like
Grandpa.
MUMMY CANNIBAL: Then just eat your
chips, dear.

Why did the cannibal feel sick after
eating the missionary?
Because you can't keep a good man down.

How can you help a starving cannibal?
Give him a hand.

What happened when the cannibals ate a
comedian?
They had a feast of fun.

Where do ghosts swim in North America?
In Lake Erie.

What kind of ghosts haunt operating
theatres?
Surgical spirits.

What brings monsters' babies?
The Frankenstork.

What did the monster say when he saw a
rush-hour train full of commuters?
'Good-oh, a chew-chew train.'

What kind of instrument does a skeleton
play?
A trom-bone.

What do you call a wicked old woman who
lives on the coast?
A sand-witch.

What do you call a nervous sorceress?
A twitch.

What do you call zombies in the belfry?
Dead ringers.

FIRST CANNIBAL: We had burglars last
    week.
SECOND CANNIBAL: Did they taste good?

FIRST CANNIBAL: Am I late for supper?
SECOND CANNIBAL: Yes, everybody's eaten.

What do young ghosts write their
    homework in?
Exorcise books.

What kind of aftershave do monsters
    wear?
Brute.

What's a sea monster's favourite food?
Fish and ships.

What did the vampire pop singer's
  admirers form?
A fang club.

Why are vampire families so close?
Because blood is thicker than water.

Why did Dracula like to help young
  vampires?
*Because he liked to get some new blood in
  the business.*

Whom did the vampire take to the
  pictures?
The girl necks door.

What is a vampire's favourite fruit?
A blood orange.

Who do cannibals eat for lunch?
Baked beings on toast.

BOILS AND BEDPANS

'Doctor, doctor, I've got a bad stomach.'
'Keep your coat buttoned up and no one will notice.'

'Doctor, doctor, I've only got fifty seconds to live.'
'Sit over there and I'll see you in a minute.'

'Doctor, doctor, can you give me something for my liver?'
'How about a pound of onions and some bacon?'

'Doctor, doctor, I feel like a wasp!'
'Buzz off!'

'Doctor, doctor, my wife keeps putting me in the dustbin.'
'Don't talk rubbish.'

'Doctor, doctor, I feel terrible. I can hardly breathe, I can't walk, and I keep getting dizzy spells and palpitations. Are you writing me a prescription?'
'No, a note for the undertaker.'

DOCTOR: I'm very sorry, Mrs Sharp, but I think you've got rabies.
MRS SHARP: Quick! Give me a piece of paper!
DOCTOR: Do you want to write your will?
MRS SHARP: No, a list of people I want to bite.

'Doctor, doctor, my hair keeps falling out. Can you give me something to keep it in?'
'You could try this carrier bag.'

DOCTOR, ANSWERING TELEPHONE: Surgery here.
MAN ON PHONE: Doctor, my wife's just dislocated her jaw. Could you come over in a month or two?

'Doctor, doctor, I feel half-dead.'
'I'll arrange for you to be buried from the waist down.'

DOCTOR: Did you drink your medicine
   after your bath?
SILLY BILLY: *No, after drinking the bath I
   didn't have room for the medicine.*

'Doctor, doctor, I'm so ugly. What can I do
   about it?'
'Hire yourself out for Hallowe'en parties.'

Did you hear about the plastic surgeon?
He sat in front of the fire and melted.

'Doctor, doctor, I think I must be invisible. Everyone ignores me.'
'*Next, please!*'

Knock, knock.
Who's there?
Money.
Money who?
Money is stiff, I hurt it playing football.

Why did the idiot burn his ear?
Someone phoned him while he was ironing.

MR BRIGHT: How long can a person live without a brain?
DOCTOR: I don't know. How old are you?

Knock, knock.
Who's there?
Ivan.
Ivan who?
Ivan infectious disease.

STINKER: Why did you leave school?
PONGO: Illness.
STINKER: Oh dear. Was it serious?
PONGO: It was the headmaster's illness.

STINKER: Why did that make you leave school?

PONGO: He got sick of me.

Why did the secretary have the ends of her fingers amputated?

So she could write shorthand.

If a young boy broke his knee, where could he get a new one?

At the butcher's, where they sell kids' knees (kidneys).

Where in Britain is spare-part surgery practised?

Liver-pool.

How do you cure acid indigestion?
Don't drink acid.

WIFE AT BEDSIDE OF SICK HUSBAND: Is there no hope, Doctor?
DOCTOR: It all depends what you are hoping for.

DOCTOR: I'm afraid you have only four minutes to live.
MRS TAWDRY: Oh dear. What shall I do?
DOCTOR: You could boil an egg.

INJURED PEDESTRIAN: What's the matter with you, are you blind?
CAR DRIVER: What do you mean, blind? I hit you, didn't I?

SNIFFY: What makes you think the surgeon doesn't like people?
NIFFY: He keeps sticking his knife into them.

What do nudists suffer from?
Clothestrophobia.

How do you make a Venetian blind?
Poke him in the eye.

'Doctor, doctor, can you give me
    something for my acne?'
'I never make rash promises.'

'Doctor, doctor, I think I need glasses.'
'You certainly do, this is an undertaker's.'

'Doctor, doctor, I want to lose thirty
    pounds excess weight.'
'Okay, I'll amputate your head.'

MRS WAYNE: I think I've got Delhi belly.
MRS WAX: I expect it's India-gestion.

DAWN: My dad can't work because Mum
broke a leg.
BRAWN: Why can't your dad work if your
mum broke a leg?
DAWN: Because she broke *his* leg.

Did you hear about the bike that went
round biting people's arms off?
It was a vicious cycle.

'Doctor, I've just been bitten on the leg by
a mad dog.'
'Did you put anything on it?'
'No, he seemed to like it as it was.'

MRS TOMCAT: And what are you going to
give your baby sister for Christmas?
PONGO: I'm not sure. Last Christmas I
gave her chickenpox.

What colour is an amputated leg?
Gang green (gangrene).

What do you call a highwayman who is
ill?
Sick Turpin.

Stinker was riding his bike round the block faster and faster, showing off to his friends. With each round he became more daring. First of all he rode round shouting, 'Look, no hands!' Then he rode round shouting, 'Look, no feet!' The third time he came round he mumbled, 'Look, no teeth!'

What should someone who wants to be an actor do?
Break a leg. Then he'll be in a cast for weeks.

'Doctor, what is the most difficult part of an operation?'
'For me, nurse, it's the sewing up. I can't see to thread the needle.'

Stinker came home from school with a stomach-ache. 'It's because your stomach's empty,' said his mum. 'If you eat your tea and fill up your stomach the pain will disappear.' And sure enough it did.

Later, his sister Selina came home from work complaining of a headache. 'It's because your head's empty,' said Stinker. 'Try putting something in it.'

MRS REEK: Why are you putting blotting paper in the baby's mouth?

RONNIE REEK: Because he's just drunk a bottle of ink.

'Doctor, doctor, I keep stealing things. Can you give me something for it?'
'Try these pills. And if they don't work, bring me back a compact disc player.'

Mr Fume was walking past a building site when a brick fell and hit him on the head. 'Oi,' he yelled, 'what do you think you're doing? You should be more careful!'

'Stop complaining,' came a voice from above. 'Look at all the bricks up here that I didn't drop!'

What did the surgeon say when he accidentally cut through a patient's artery?
'Aorta know better.'

'Nurse, nurse, I'm at death's door.'
'Don't worry, Mrs Ratbag, the doctor will pull you through.'

'I told you not to swallow,' shouted the irate dentist. 'That was my last pair of pliers.'

'Doctor, doctor, I've got such a headache.'
'Put your head through the window and the pain will disappear.'

'Doctor, doctor, my kidneys are bad. What should I do?'
'Take them back to the butcher's.'

'Doctor, doctor, little Jimmy has a saucepan stuck on his head. Whatever shall I do?'
'Don't worry, you can borrow one of mine. I'm going out for dinner.'

'Doctor, am I going to get well? My friend told me about a doctor treating someone for bronchitis and they died of a heart attack!'
'Don't worry, Mr Stench, if I treat someone for bronchitis they die of bronchitis.'

'Doctor, doctor, I'm having trouble with my breathing.'
'I'll give you something that will soon stop that.'

'Doctor, doctor, I can't keep my food down. Everything I swallow comes up.'
'Quick, swallow my premium bond.'

'Doctor, doctor, I tend to flush a lot.'
'Don't worry, it's just a normal chain reaction.'

'Doctor, doctor, I've just swallowed a mouth organ.'
'Be thankful you don't play a grand piano.'

74

'Doctor, doctor, everyone thinks I'm a liar.'
'I don't believe you.'

What did one germ say to the other?
'Keep away, I've caught penicillin.'

A man came round in hospital after having an eye operation to find the surgeon standing by his bed. 'How did the operation go?' he enquired weakly.

'Well,' replied the surgeon, 'I'm pleased to say we managed to save your eye. We'll give it to you as a souvenir when you leave.'

JULES: How did you break your leg?
DROOLS: You see those steps at the side of the garage?
JULES: Yes.
DROOLS: Well, I didn't.

VICKY: You're looking a little pale.
STICKY: I've been ill. I nearly kicked the bucket.

Stinker was climbing a tree and had nearly reached the top when his mother came into the garden and saw him. She shouted up, 'If you fall and break both legs, don't come running to me, that's all!'

Mrs Tawdry had had a face-lift, the extra skin being taken from her bottom. Her friend Mrs Stench asked her how she was. 'Well,' she replied, 'I feel all right, but when I get tired my face wants to sit down.'

DOCTOR: Well, Mr Tipple, I can't find anything wrong with you. It must be the drink.

MR TIPPLE: Okay, Doctor, I'll come back in the morning when you're sober.

'Doctor, doctor, what did the X-ray of my head show?'

'*Absolutely nothing, Mr Polecat.*'

'Doctor, doctor, I've got a button up my nose. What should I do?'

'*Just breathe through the four little holes.*'

'Doctor, I think I have a split personality.'

'*One patient at a time, please.*'

'Doctor, doctor, I'm such a mess. I think I must have an inferiority complex.'

'*Nonsense. You are inferior.*'

Mr Tawdry had been prescribed two pounds of carrots a day for his bad eyesight. After he'd been on his diet for a month he returned to the surgery covered in bruises.

'What's the matter?' asked the doctor. 'Didn't the diet work? Isn't your eyesight better?'

'It's much better,' replied Mr Tawdry, 'but the trouble is, I keep falling over my ears.'

'Doctor, how can I stop walking in my sleep?'
'Put some tin tacks on the floor.'

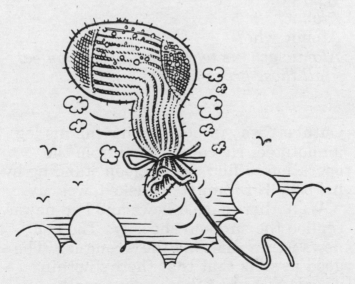

Mrs Pigsfeet had just had her appendix removed. Dr Carver came to ask the nurse how she was. 'She seems well,' replied the nurse, 'but when I listened to her chest, she seemed to have two heartbeats.'

'Ah,' said Dr Carver, 'I wondered what had happened to my watch.'

DOCTOR: Please breathe out three times.
MR FEATHER: Why, do you want to check my lungs?
DOCTOR: No, I want to clean my glasses.

Knock, knock.
Who's there?
Atomic.
Atomic who?
Atomic ache is what you'll get if you eat all those green apples.

Cuthbert was in hospital having his leg amputated. He came round from the operation to find the surgeon standing by his bed. 'How am I?' he asked, wearily.

'Well, there's good news and bad news,' replied the surgeon cheerily. 'The bad news is, we removed the wrong leg. The good news is that that there's nothing wrong with the other one after all.'

CRUEL CRACKS

BARBER: Were you wearing a red scarf when you came in?
CUSTOMER: No.
BARBER: Oh dear. I must have cut your throat.

STINKER: Do you still hold your girlfriend's hand?
PONGO: Yes, but I wish the rest of her would visit me more often.

INSURANCE SALESMAN: This is a very good policy, sir. We pay £1000 for a broken arm or leg.
MR DIMWIT: What on earth do you do with them?

What does an executioner do with a
notepad and a pencil?
Writes his chopping list.

'Mummy, Mummy, Daddy just fell off the
    ladder!'
*'I know, darling, I saw him go past the
    window.'*

'Mummy, Mummy, I don't want to go to
    America!'
'Shut up and keep swimming!'

DETECTIVE: Your first two wives died after
    eating poisoned ham sandwiches, and
    your third has just broken her neck after
    falling off the roof. It's all rather
    suspicious, isn't it?
HUSBAND: Not really. She wouldn't eat the
    poisoned sandwiches.

NIFFY: Can you lend me ten pence? I want
    to phone a friend.
WHIFFY: Here's twenty pence. Phone all of
    them.

A man with a large dog walked into a
pub. 'Do you serve people who haven't
changed their socks for a month?' he
asked.
    The barman was horrified. But the dog
was pretty big, so he thought he had
better be polite.
    'Er, of course we do,' he replied.
    'Right,' said the man with the dog. 'A

pint for me, and a person who hasn't changed his socks for a month for Rover here, please!'

VICKY: We had Auntie Mabel for lunch last Sunday.
STICKY: Really? We had roast beef.

FIRST TOURIST: Don't swim in that sea. A shark just bit off my foot!
SECOND TOURIST: Which one?
FIRST TOURIST: How should I know? All sharks look the same to me.

JACQUI: Why did you come home early from your farm holiday?
TACQUI: The first day we were there a duck died, so we had roast duck for dinner. The second day a calf died, so we had veal cutlets. The third day the cowman died . . .

BORIS: Say you'll marry me, or I'll blow my brains out.
DORIS: Go ahead – you've not much to lose.

'They say Grandad has one foot in the grate.'
'Don't you mean "one foot in the grave"?'
'No, the grate. He wants to be cremated.'

'Archibald! Why did you put that slug in your aunt's bed?'
'Because I couldn't find a cobra.'

SIGN IN A BARBER'S SHOP: Hair cut for £2.50. Children for £1.50.

WINIFRED: Why can't I go swimming, Mummy?
MOTHER: Because there are sharks in the sea.
WINIFRED: But Daddy's swimming.
MOTHER: That's different, he's insured.

MOTHER: Why are you crying, Clarence?
CLARENCE: All the children at school call me Bighead.
MOTHER: Don't worry, Clarence. Just pop round to the greengrocer's and get me three pounds of potatoes in your cap.

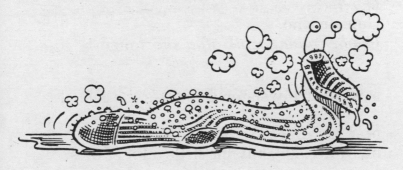

Pongo couldn't swim, and was floundering around in the river. As he came up for the third time, his friend Stinker called from the bank, 'If you drown, can I have your BMX bike?'

Mr Wally was in the divorce court, trying to divorce his wife, Mrs Wally, on the grounds that she smoked in bed.

'That doesn't sound too serious,' said the judge.

'But she doesn't smoke cigarettes, m'lud,' replied Mr Wally. 'She smokes kippers.'

SIDNEY SNOOTY: One of my ancestors died at Waterloo.
OLLIE ORDINARY: Really? Was it caused by eating British Rail sandwiches?

Knock, knock.
Who's there?
Gopher.
Gopher who?
Gopher a long walk off a short pier.

DESMOND: My sister Deirdre's the school swot.
DILBERT: Does she do well in exams?
DESMOND: No, but she kills a lot of flies.

MRS MOUSETROUSER: Why are you home from school so early, Maurice?

MAURICE MOUSETROUSER: I was sent home because Arthur was smoking.

MRS MOUSETROUSER: If Arthur was smoking why were you sent home?

MAURICE MOUSETROUSER: It was me who set him on fire.

Who is the meanest person in the world?
A man who finds a sling and then breaks his arm to wear it.

A taxi driver found a carrier bag full of chicken giblets in his cab and took it to the police.
They told him that if no one had claimed it after six months it would be his.

Why did his friends call Edgar 'Camembert'?
They were cheesed off by the smell of his feet.

Did you know that two out of three people are mad? Check your friends: if they are all right, it must be you.

SALLY: Why do they call your brother Wonder Boy?

WALLY: Because people look at him and wonder.

RONALD: Did you miss me when I was away?

ROBINA: Were you away?

WILFRED: Why doesn't your sister wear lipstick?

WILLOUGHBY: She can't keep her mouth still long enough to put it on.

SALESMAN AT DOOR: Does your husband have life insurance?

WOMAN OF HOUSE: No, just fire insurance. He knows where he's going.

PENELOPE: You remind me of the sea.

PEREGRINE: Why? Because I'm wild and free and romantic?

PENELOPE: No, because you make me sick.

CYNTHIA: Whisper something soft and sweet in my ear.

CORNELIUS: Melting ice-cream.

MRS PUTRID: I'm sorry, dear, but the dog ate your dinner.
MR PUTRID: Don't worry, I'll buy you another dog.

CUSTOMER: I'd like a mousetrap, please.
CHEMIST: Have you tried Boots?
CUSTOMER: I'd like to catch it, not kick it to death.

What happened when two fat men ran in a race?
One ran in short bursts, the other ran in burst shorts.

MRS CREAK: The new baby is the image of his father.
MRS REEK: Never mind, just as long as it's healthy.

Did you hear what happened when Stinker
    went to see a mind-reader?
They gave him his money back.

'I wouldn't say he was filthy, but his
clothes get dirtier on the inside than on the
outside.'

MRS RAT-TRAP: Stop reaching across the
    table like that. Haven't you got a
    tongue?
REGGIE RAT-TRAP: Yes, Mum, but my arm is
    longer.

SIGN OUTSIDE A BACON-SLICING FACTORY:
    Extra hands needed.

PONGO: I think my mum's trying to get rid
    of me. Every time she wraps up my
    packed lunch she puts a road map in it.

'I wouldn't say she was ugly, but when a
wasp stings her it closes its eyes.'

When Stinker sent his picture to a lonely
hearts club they sent it back. They said
they weren't that lonely.

EDIE: I see you're wearing your Easter shirt.
SEEDY: Why do you call it my Easter shirt?
EDIE: Because it's covered in egg.

CYRIL: Is that perfume I smell?
CLARISSA: It is, and you do.

CLOGGY: If frozen water is iced water, what is frozen ink?
SOGGY: Iced ink.
CLOGGY: You sure do!

SAMANTHA: I have music in my feet!
SAMSON: Yes, two flats.

MRS TUM: I got these trousers for an absurd price.
MRS BUM: You mean for a ridiculous figure!

PONGO: It's nearly my birthday, Dad, and I've got my eye on a lovely new bike.
PONGO'S DAD: Well, you'd better keep your eye on it, son, because you'll never get your bottom on it!

'In future, Lucinda, please sing only Christmas carols. Then we'll have to listen to you only once a year.'

MRS BROOM: What a filthy mess you look, Arabella!
ARABELLA: Sorry, Mum, I fell in a cow pat.
MRS BROOM: What, in your new dress?
ARABELLA: But, Mum, I didn't have time to change.

How did the carpenter regain his sight?
He picked up his hammer and saw.

What time is it when you sit on a pin?
Spring time.

'Are you superstitious?'
'No.'
'Then lend me £13.'

'Mum, is it true that the new baby came from heaven?'
'Yes, dear.'
'Well, I don't blame them for throwing him out.'

BEN: Can Darren come out to play?
MRS BARROW: No, he's ill in bed.
BEN: Well, er, could his football come out to play then?

Happy birthday to you,
Squashed tomatoes and stew,
Bread and butter in the gutter,
Happy birthday to you.

'No, Charlotte, you may not borrow the
  hammer. You'll hurt your fingers.'
'No I won't, Dad. Young Henry is going to
  hold the nails for me.'

Mother was amazed at the generosity
shown by Dirty Bertie to his little friend,

Annie, when he let Annie have first go on
his new ice skates. 'That was very kind of
you, Bertie,' she said.

'That's all right, Mum,' replied Bertie.
'I'm waiting to see if the ice is thick
enough.'

HORACE: Dad, there's a boy in my class who
    says I look just like you.
DAD: What did you say to him, son?
HORACE: Nothing. He's bigger than me.

ARAMINTA: Mummy, Mummy, Cyril's
    broken my favourite dolly.
MUMMY: Naughty boy! How did he do that?
ARAMINTA: I hit him over the head with it.

Mrs Flannel was shopping in the
supermarket with her baby, Freddie, when
she started to cry.

'What's the matter, love?' asked a kindly
check-out girl.

'It's that woman over there. She said my
son Freddie was ugly.'

'Well, don't cry. Look, I'm going off duty
now. Come and have a cup of tea with me.
And while we're about it, what about a
banana for the monkey?'

MOTHER: Why are you crying?
TRACY: I fell down and grazed my knee.
MOTHER: When was that?
TRACY: Half an hour ago when I was out
     playing.
MOTHER: But I didn't hear you crying then.
TRACY: No, I thought you were out.

Little Felicity was being extra nice to Aunt
Dahlia, who rarely came on a visit.
    'I do believe you don't want me to go,'
said Aunt Dahlia.
    'You're right,' said Felicity. ''Cos Dad
says that as soon as you've gone he's going
to give me a good hiding.'

'How did Mum know you hadn't had a
     bath?'
'I forgot to wet the soap.'

'Did you hear about Sharon? She got
    engaged to Albert, and then found he'd
    got a wooden leg!'
'Good heavens! What did she do?'
'What could she do? She broke it off, of
    course.'

What did the speak-your-weight machine
    say when the large lady stepped on it?
'One at a time, please.'

The bus was full and three women had to
stand up. A very fat woman who was
sitting down leaned over to a man opposite
and said, 'If you were a gentleman you'd
stand up and let one of these ladies sit
down.'
    He replied, 'And if you were a lady you'd
stand up and let all three of them sit down!'

What did the verger say when the church
was on fire?
'Holy smoke!'

What do you get if you cross the Atlantic
with the *Titanic*?
Half-way.

'Mummy, Mummy, why can't we have a
   dustbin?'
'Shut up and keep chewing.'

'Daddy, Daddy, I don't want to go to
   Australia!'
'Shut up and keep digging.'

'I wouldn't say Basil was insensitive, but
he did walk into a crematorium and ask
what was cooking!'

'I wouldn't say Lizzie was thin but when
she drinks tomato juice she looks like a
thermometer.'

'Harold goes to the dentist twice a year —
once for each tooth.'

STINKER: Why does your sister wear so
   much make-up?
PONGO: What makes you ask?
STINKER: I saw her at the cinema last night
   and her face was still smiling five
   minutes after she'd stopped laughing.

What's the penalty for bigamy?
Two mothers-in-law.

MAN IN FABRIC SHOP: I'd like two yards of satan for my wife, please.
ASSISTANT: You mean satin; satan is something that looks like the devil.
MAN: Oh, you've seen my wife, then?

'Audrey's mum said you and Dad weren't fit to live with pigs.'
'And what did you say?'
'I stuck up for you. I said of course you were.'

VISITOR: You're very quiet, Andrew.
ANDREW: Mum gave me twenty pence not to say anything about your cross eyes.

ALICE: I've changed my mind.
ALETHEA: Does the new one work any better?

SUSIE: Boys keep telling me I'm beautiful.
SALLY: Some people have a vivid imagination.

MR STICKY: My wife has an impediment in her speech. Every now and then she has to stop to breathe.

BESSIE: I'm thinking hard.
JESSIE: You mean it's hard for you to think!

When a photographer took Boris's
   photograph he never developed it.
*He was afraid of being alone in the dark
   with it.*

MRS WACKY: Why don't you go and play
   cowboys and Indians with Grandad?
JACKIE WACKY: He's no use. He's been
   scalped already.

Knock, knock.
Who's there?
Philippa.
Philippa who?
Philippa bath, I'm very dirty.

MR BULL: Excuse me, I think you're sitting in my seat.

MR DULL: Can you prove it's your seat?

MR BULL: I certainly can. I left a bag of kippers on it.

Mr Coldhead was buying a new hat. He was offered various types – a bowler, a cap, a panama – but didn't like any of them. Finally the assistant had a brainwave. 'How about a pork pie hat?' he asked. 'That would look nice.'

'Oh, no,' replied Mr Coldhead. 'I've had one of those before, and I couldn't stand the way the gravy kept running down my neck.'

STINKER: When I was little we were so poor we couldn't have a sledge when it snowed.

PONGO: What did you do?

STINKER: I used to slide down hills on my little brother.

JACQUI: When *I* was little we were so poor we ate only one meal a week.

TACQUI: So what? *We* were so poor we had only one pimple at a time!

GRANDMA: I wouldn't slide down the
    banisters like that if I were you, Freddie.
FREDDIE: How would you slide down them,
    Gran?

AUDREY: Do you always bathe in muddy
    water?
TAWDRY: It wasn't muddy when I got in.

Look at her feet –
She thinks she's neat:
Long black stockings
And dirty feet.

BERTHA: My sister can play the piano by
    ear.
BASIL: So what? My brother fiddles with his
    toes.

MOTHER: Harold! What did you say to
    Bessie to make her cry?
HAROLD: I paid her a compliment.
MOTHER: And what was that?
HAROLD: I told her she sweated less than
    any girl I'd ever danced with.

FATHER: Who broke that window?
DARREN: Ben did. He ducked when I threw
    a cricket ball at him.

MABEL: When I'm old and ugly, will you
    still love me?
PERCY: I do, don't I?

GILLIE: Will I lose my looks as I get older?
WILLIE: With luck, yes.

Knock, knock.
Who's there?
Alec.
Alec who?
Alec Veronica but I don't like you.

**Why did the millionaire live in a mansion
    without a bathroom?**
He was filthy rich.

'Is it polite to eat sweetcorn with your
    fingers?'
'No, fingers should be eaten separately.'

EXAMINER: Can you quote a passage from
    the Bible, Cynthia?
CYNTHIA: 'Judas departed, and went and
    hanged himself.'
EXAMINER: Good. And can you quote
    another?
CYNTHIA: 'Go thou and do likewise.'

HUMPHREY: What's that perfume called?
HANNAH: 'High Heaven'.
HUMPHREY: It certainly smells to it!

Knock, knock.
Who's there?
Paul Aidy.
Paul Aidy who?
*Paul Aidy, Stinker just pushed her over in
    the mud.*

Why didn't Bessie Bunter's facelift work?
The crane broke.

IRATE CUSTOMER: I didn't come here to be
    insulted!
SHOP ASSISTANT: Where do you usually go?

Why did the woman wear sunglasses whenever she looked at her husband? *Because he was so bald the reflected light hurt her eyes.*

Little Jane had taken up pressing flowers and was busy picking pretty, sweet-scented flowers to put in her album. Her mother came out to see what she was doing, and discovered her brother Pongo busy collecting things out of the vegetable patch.

'What are you doing, Pongo?' she asked.

'Collecting slugs, Mum,' he replied.

'And what are you going to do with them?'

'Press them with Jane's flowers.'

STAN: I have a hunch.

ANNE: I always thought you were round-shouldered.

SAMANTHA WARBLE: What would you like me to sing next?

MEMBER OF AUDIENCE: Do you know 'Loch Lomond'?

SAMANTHA WARBLE: Yes.

MEMBER OF AUDIENCE: Well, go and jump in it.

Stinker was amazed at the age of his great-grandfather. 'Were you in the Ark with Noah?' he asked.

'Of course not,' replied Great-grandfather.

'Then why didn't you drown?' asked Stinker.

What happened when the joker dropped a
    grand piano down a mine shaft?
He got A flat miner.

What did mean Mervyn do when his house
    was on fire?
Prayed for rain.

One afternoon at school there was a
    terrible thunderstorm.
*The word went round the class that the
    physics teacher was doing experiments
    again.*

GREASY SPOONS

STINKER: I know a café where we can eat
   dirt cheap.
PONGO: But who wants to eat dirt?

What's white outside, grey and slimy
   inside, and moves very slowly?
A slug sandwich.

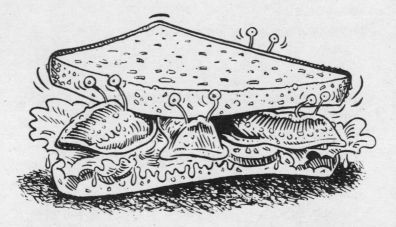

What's the difference between frogspawn
   and tapioca pudding?
Not a lot.

WAITER: Soup's off today, sir.
DINER: I'll say it is. Mine had green mould on it.

DINER: How often do you change the tablecloths in this establishment?
WAITER: I don't know, sir, I've only worked here six months.

DINER: Waiter, there's no chicken in this chicken pie.
WAITER: There are no shepherds in the shepherd's pie, either, sir.

Which town in Britain makes terrible sandwiches?
Oldham.

What kind of salad speaks for itself?
A tongue salad.

A tramp was begging for food. 'Didn't I give you a bowl of curry last week?' asked Mrs Rumbleguts.

'Yes, ma'am,' replied the tramp. 'But I've recovered now.'

What happened to the woman who
   dreamed she was eating a giant
   marshmallow?
She woke to find her pillow had
   disappeared.

Knock, knock.
Who's there?
Aida.
Aida who?
Aida thirty-two chocolate bars and now I
   feel terrible.

Should you eat ten cream doughnuts on an empty stomach?
It's better to eat them on a plate.

CORONER: And what were your wife's last words, Mr Weed?
MR WEED: They were: 'I don't see how they can make a profit selling this salmon at 2p a tin'.

'Waiter! There's a fly in my soup!'
'Yes, sir, it's the bad meat that attracts them.'

'Waiter! There's a fly in my soup!'
'Don't worry, sir, the tarantula on the roll will catch it.'

'Waiter! There's a fly in my alphabet soup!'
'I expect it's learning to read, sir.'

'Waiter! There's a fly in my soup!'
'That's the manager, sir. The last customer was a witch doctor.'

'Waiter! There's a fly in my wine!'
'Well, you did ask for something with a little body, sir.'

'Waiter, was this dish called cottage pie?'
'Yes, sir.'
'Well, call a doctor. I think I've just eaten the drains.'

'Waiter, this food is disgusting. Get me the manager!'
'It's no use, sir, he thinks it's disgusting, too.'

Mrs Wax and Mrs Wayne were discussing a meal they had eaten recently with an acquaintance who was a very bad cook. 'And that salmon!' exclaimed Mrs Wax.
    'That wasn't salmon,' explained Mrs Wayne. 'That was cod blushing at the mess she'd made of it.'

'I wouldn't say my mum is a bad cook, but ours is the only dustbin in the street with indigestion.'

SIGN IN BUTCHER'S SHOP: John Brown butchers pigs like his father.

MRS MOAN: How was your supper, dear?
MR MOAN: The meat was so tough I couldn't get my fork into the gravy.

'Mummy, Mummy, what's a vampire?'
'Shut up and drink your tomato juice before it clots.'

What does a professor of anatomy eat with cheese?
Pickled organs.

Why did the orchestra player live on baked beans?
So he could play the Trumpet Voluntary.

Did you hear the Department of Energy is experimenting with wind power?
They all eat ten cans of baked beans a day.

SIGN IN HEALTH FOOD STORE: Closed because of illness.

MR BIGBELLY: This tea tastes like used bath water.
MRS BIGBELLY: How would you know?

'Waiter! This coffee tastes like mud!'
'It was ground this morning, sir.'

MRS SLACK: This tea is terrible.
MR SLACK: I made it in my pyjamas.
MRS SLACK: No wonder it tastes so bad.

STINKER: I live on garlic alone.
PONGO: Anyone who lives on garlic should live alone.

'Waiter! Has this salad been washed?'
'It certainly has. You can still see the soap in it.'

What was the western sheriff who lived on pickled onions called?
Wyatt Burp.

MAN AT DINNER PARTY: My wife eats likes a bird.
HOSTESS: You mean she likes small helpings?
MAN AT DINNER PARTY: No, she likes a plateful of worms and slugs.

111

What's worse than finding a slug in a
   strawberry that you're eating?
Finding half a slug in it.

'Waiter! Do you serve crabs?'
'Sit down, sir, we serve anybody.'

WAITER: We have everything on the menu,
   sir.
DINER: So I see. Please bring me a clean
   one.

LIME: Eat up your greens.
LEMON: But I don't like greens, Lime.

Why was the tomato red?
Because it saw the salad dressing.

What is rhubarb?
Embarrassed celery.

There were two provisions shops next door
to one another. One put up a sign:
WE SELL OUR PORK PIES TO THE QUEEN. The
next day the other put up a sign:
GOD SAVE THE QUEEN.

'Waiter! There's a hand in my soup!'
*'That's not your soup, sir, it's the finger
bowl.'*

Why is a cottage like meals eaten on a sea
crossing?
Two down, two up.

There were two boiled eggs in a pan. One
said, 'Phew, it's hot in here!'
The other replied, 'It gets worse. When
you get out they smash your head in.'

When Lee ate raw onions for a week what
did he become?
Lone Lee.

What's yellow, brown, and hairy?
Cheese on toast dropped on the carpet.

'Waiter! What's this soup?'
'It's bean soup, sir.'
'I don't care what it's been, what is it now?'

What happened when the carrot died?
There was a huge turnip at the funeral.

Did you hear the joke about the three eggs?
Two bad.

Pongo's dad was late home. 'Did you keep my supper warm?' he asked Pongo's mum.
   'Yes, dear,' she replied. 'The cat's been sitting on it all evening.'

'Waiter! Why is my steak pie all mashed up?'
'Well, you did ask me to step on it, sir.'

'Waiter! What are these two worms on my plate?'
'Your sausages, sir.'

'Are you sure this ham is cured? It tastes
as if it's still sick!'

CLARISSA: Are slugs nice to eat, Miss?
TEACHER: Clarissa! Get on with your dinner
and stop asking disgusting questions at
the table!
TEACHER (later, when dinner was over): Now,
Clarissa, what was it you wanted to ask
me?
CLARISSA: Oh, it doesn't matter now, Miss.
There was a slug on your salad but it had
vanished by the end of the meal.

Did you hear about the impatient man who
went to a fish and chip shop and ordered
shark and chips? He asked the proprietor
to make it snappy.

Why was the restaurant called 'Out of This
World'?
It was full of Unidentified Frying Objects.

'Waiter, what's wrong with this fish?'
'Long time, no sea, sir.'

DINER: I'll have the tomato soup followed by the cod steak.
WAITER: I'd have the fish first if I were you, sir.
DINER: Why's that?
WAITER: It's on the turn.

'Waiter! This chicken's very oily!'
'Yes, sir, it's a slick chick.'

'Waiter! This bun tastes of soap!'
'It's a Bath bun, sir.'

'Waiter! This tea tastes like paraffin!'
'You should try the coffee, sir. It tastes like petrol.'

The teacher asked if everyone was enjoying the school dinner.
'The meat's very tough,' replied Pongo. The teacher came over and took a piece off the side of his plate and chewed it.
'Nonsense, Pongo,' she said. 'It seems perfectly all right to me.'
'It may be *now*, Miss,' said Pongo, 'but I've been chewing it for the last twenty minutes!'

DOWN THE DRAIN

What kind of tree grows near volcanoes?
A lava tree (lavatory).

What is an ig?
An Eskimo house without a loo.

Why do traffic lights turn red?
Because they have to stop and go in the middle of the road.

What kind of nut do you find in the loo?
A peanut.

What dashed round the desert on a camel carrying a bedpan?
Florence of Arabia.

STINKER: You have to be a good singer in our house.
PONGO: Why's that?
STINKER: There's no lock on the loo door.

118

Knock, knock.
Who's there?
Butter.
Butter who?
Butter be quick, I need the loo desperately.

On the road from Dover a French hitch-hiker thumbed a lift. A motorist stopped. 'Do you want a lift?' he asked.

'Oui, oui,' replied the hitch-hiker.

'Not in my car you don't,' said the motorist firmly, and drove off.

What's the dirtiest word in the world?
Pollution.

What's wet, black, floats on water, and shouts 'Knickers!'?
Crude oil.

What's wet, black, floats on water, and shouts 'Underwear!'?
Refined oil.

Did you hear about the girl who bought a
    pair of paper knickers?
She didn't like them; they were tear-able.

What do you call two policemen?
A pair of navy blue knickers.

Knock, knock.
Who's there?
Euripides.
Euripides who?
Euripides you pay for a new pair.

Knock, knock.
Who's there?
Nick.
Nick who?
Nick R. Elastic.

Lady Nobbleknees was giving her servant
a telling off. 'You must not come into my
bedroom or my bathroom without
knocking, Charles,' she said.
    'It's all right, ma'am,' he replied. 'Before I
come in I always look through the keyhole,
and if you have nothing on I don't come in.'

Who lived in the woods and told dirty jokes to wolves?
Little Rude Riding Hood.

MAN IN SHOP: May I try on those red
   swimming trunks in the window?
ASSISTANT: No – you'll have to go in the
   changing room like everyone else.

MR TAWDRY: We've been in Paris four days
   and we haven't visited the Louvre yet.
MRS TAWDRY: I expect it's the change in the
   water.

How do you get a paper baby?
Marry an old bag.

What do men do standing up, women do
   sitting down, and dogs do on three legs?
Shake hands.

What was the rude saint called?
Nicholas (knicker-less).

Knock, knock.
Who's there?
Kipper.
Kipper who?
Kipper your hands to yourself.

What's brown and sounds like a bell?
Dung.

Jules received an invitation to an Adam
   and Eve party.
It said: 'Leaves off at eleven.'

IDA: Would you like to hear a poem?
SPIDER: I only like poems that rhyme.
IDA: This one goes:
   There was a young lady called Nellie,
   Who fell in the water up to her knees . . .
SPIDER: That doesn't rhyme!
IDA: I'm afraid the water wasn't deep
   enough.

Why can't a steam engine sit down?
Because it has a tender behind.

What shoots, makes tracks, and should be
   cleaned with disinfectant?
A septic tank.

Knock, knock.
Who's there?
Luke.
Luke who?
*Luke through the keyhole and you'll see
   auntie in her underwear.*

Knock, knock.
Who's there?
Pencil.
Pencil who?
Pencil fall down if your braces snap.

STINKER: Why was your little brother locked up on the ship?
PONGO: Well, he thought the poop deck was the place to go.

JENNY: What would you do if you were camping in the Rocky Mountains, and had just got into your tent and taken all your clothes off to go to bed when a grizzly bear came up behind you?
PENNY: Run!
JENNY: What, with a bear behind?

MR SEEDY: I've just bought my wife a bottle of toilet water. It cost me £20!
MR WEEDY: £20! You could have come round to our house and had some out of our toilet for nothing.

Why was the silly man expelled from the committee meeting?
He passed the wrong sort of motion.

NEWSFLASH: A hole has been discovered in the fence around Coldflesh Nudist Camp. Police are looking into it.

Why did the maths teacher hide under the
    bed?
Because he thought he was a little potty.

Veronica was saying her alphabet for the
teacher. 'A, B, C . . .' she began, 'L, M, N, O,
Q, P . . .'
    Her teacher interrupted. 'No, no,
Veronica, P comes before Q.'
    'When we went on our school outing,
Miss,' said the erring pupil, 'queue *always*
came before pee.'

NEWSPAPER HEADLINE: Christmas babies
flood local hospital.

EXTRACT FROM THE DOVER ADVERTISER: Due
to industrial action holiday-makers spent
eight hours waiting for the jerry. When it
did arrive it was filled to capacity.

MR STENCH, PEERING OVER GARDEN FENCE:
    What are you going to do with that pile
    of manure?
MR PONG: Put it on my strawberries.
MR STENCH: Really? I put cream on mine.

A scout group were on an orienteering
course, and one of them, Silly Willy, was

very late back at the camp. 'William!' roared the scoutmaster, 'what happened to you?'

'Sir,' replied Willy. 'You know that field of cows we went through? Well, my beret blew off, and I had to try on twenty before I found it.'

What has two legs, one wheel, and stinks
   to high heaven?
A barrowload of manure.

What's brown, smelly, and goes round and
   round?
A long-playing cow pat.

Why do babies gurgle with joy?
Because babyhood is such a nappy time.

The Whiff and Sniff Corporation's lift shot very quickly down the shaft when the managing director was in it. 'Did I go too fast, sir?' enquired the lift operator.

'No,' scowled the MD. 'I always go home with my trousers round my ankles.'

SNUFFBOX

Why was the graveyard so noisy?
Because of the coffin.

How can you tell when a corpse is angry?
It flips its lid.

Where do undertakers go in October?
The Hearse of the Year Show.

How do undertakers speak?
Gravely.

When can't you bury people who live
   opposite a graveyard?
When they're not dead.

MRS SLIMY: When my Albert dies they're
   going to bury him face down.
MRS SLITHER: Why?
MRS SLIMY: So he can see where he's going.

What was written on the hypochondriac's
   tombstone?
'I told you I was ill.'

What is a drunkard's last drink?
His bier.

Her death it brought us bitter woe,
Yea, to the heart it wrung us.
And all because she didn't know
A mushroom from a fungus.

What was proved when the fat man was
   run over by a steam-roller?
That he had a lot of guts.

What were Batman and Robin called after
   they'd been run over by a steam-roller?
Flatman and Ribbon.

He passed the lorry without any fuss,
And he passed the cart of hay;
He tried to pass a swerving bus –
And then he passed away.

What were Tarzan's last words?
'Who greased that vine?'

How can you get to heaven quickly?
Jump out of an express train.

Did you hear about the man who believed
   in reincarnation?
In his will he left his money to himself.

JULES: Last week my dad went to the
   garden to pick some carrots for dinner,
   had a heart attack, and died.
DROOLS: How awful! What did your mother
   do?
JULES: What could she do? She opened a
   packet of frozen peas.

Did you hear about the man who jumped in
   the River Thames?
He committed sewercide.

FIRST BURGLAR: Quick! The police! Jump
   out of the window!
SECOND BURGLAR: But we're on the
   thirteenth floor!
FIRST BURGLAR: This is no time for
   superstition.

STINKER: My grandmother fell down the
   stairs.
PONGO: Cellar?
STINKER: No, we think she can be repaired.

TEACHER: Name a deadly poison.
CUTHBERT: Aviation.
TEACHER: Aviation?
CUTHBERT: Yes, sir, one drop and you're
dead.

What did the executioner's wife say to
him?
*'There are only ten chopping days to
Christmas.'*

Class 2A was on a ferry bound for France, and the head teacher was checking on the safety procedures. 'What do you do if a boy falls overboard?' he asked the children.

'Shout "boy overboard", sir,' replied Biggins.

'Right,' said the Head. 'And what do you do if a teacher falls overboard?'

'Er, well, sir, which one?' replied Biggins.

What happened when Lucy pushed her
    father's fingers in the light socket?
She got fizzy pop.

CLASSIFIED ADVERTISEMENT: For sale. 1926
    hearse. Excellent condition; original
    body.

When do you get that run-down feeling?
When you've been hit by a car.

How can you make a thin person fat?
*Push him over a cliff and he'll come down
    plump.*

Why did the man jump off the top of the
    Empire State Building?
*Because he wanted to make a hit on
    Broadway.*

How do you tell an undertaker?
By his grave manner.

Did you hear about the Chinese waiter who
   got fed up?
He committed chop sueycide.

FARMER: Where's that mare I told you to
   get shod?
DIM DENNIS: Did you say 'shod'? I thought
   you said 'shot'.

Mr and Mrs Twistleton were on safari in
Africa. A large lion grabbed Mr Twistleton
in its massive jaws. 'Shoot, shoot!' he cried
to his wife.
   'I can't,' she cried, 'I've run out of film.'

A lady who came from Kilbride
Ate so many apples she died.
The apples fermented
Inside the lamented,
Making cider inside 'er inside.

What did one worm in the graveyard say to
   the other?
*'I have something to tell you in dead
   Ernest.'*

Did you hear about the painter who died
   after drinking a tin of varnish?
He has a lovely finish.

VICKY: I hear you buried your auntie last
   week.
STICKY: Had to. She was dead, you know.

What happened to the boat that sank in
   the sea full of piranha fish?
It came back with a skeleton crew.

NERVOUS PASSENGER: How often do planes of this type crash?
CAPTAIN: Only once, Madam.

She stood on the bridge at midnight,
Her lips were all a-quiver.
She gave a cough, her leg fell off,
And floated down the river.

What should you take when you're
knocked down by a car?
Its registration number.

TILLY: Do you know someone is killed in a road accident every two minutes?
WILLY: I bet he gets awfully tired of it.

A boy on a bike knocked into an old lady.
'Don't you know how to ride a bike?' she squealed.
'Yes, but I don't know how to work the bell.'

What do you have to take to become a
coroner?
A stiff exam.

What goes ho, ho, ho, plop?
Santa Claus laughing his head off.

Why didn't Pongo think much of the knife-
throwing act at the fair?
Because the thrower never hit the girl once.

'Grandad, do you know how to croak?'
'I don't think so, Stanley, why?'
'Because Dad says he'll be rich when you
    do.'

What do you do if you laugh until your
    sides split?
Run until you get a stitch.

Out in the Wild West a cowboy found an
Indian with his ear pressed to the ground.
'What are you listening for?' asked the
cowboy.
   'A stage coach passed this way five
minutes ago,' said the Indian.
   'How can you tell?' asked the cowboy.
   'It broke my neck,' replied the Indian.

A man fell over a cliff and broke both arms.
His rescuer dangled a rope down and told
him to catch hold of it in his teeth while he
hauled him up. Inch by inch the man was
pulled up the cliff, until he was only six
feet from the top. 'Are you okay?' shouted
the rescuer.
   'Yeeeeeee – heeeelllllllppppp!' came the
reply.

JUDGE: And why did you stab your wife ninety-nine times, Mr Edwards?

MR EDWARDS: I forgot to switch off the electric carving knife.

'And how did you have your accident?'

'You know the sign by the railway that says "Stop, Look, and Listen"?'

'Yes.'

'Well, I was doing that when the train hit me.'

'Quick, quick, get the doctor. I think Granny's taken a turn for the hearse.'

MR SMITH: My wife's an angel.

MR JONES: I'm sorry to hear that. Mine's still alive.

Mr Pop and Mr Gunn were out shooting.

'Oi,' said Mr Pop, 'you nearly shot my wife!'

'Sorry,' replied Mr Gunn. 'Shall I have another go?'

What's black and white, and goes moo, moo, splat?

A cow falling over a cliff.

Mr Jones was sent by his company to Africa to sell refrigerators. When he had settled in at his hotel, he sent a telegram to his wife, as he knew she'd be worried about him.

Unfortunately the telegram was delivered to another Mrs Jones, whose husband had just died. It read: 'Arrived safely. The heat is terrible!'

What do you get if you are hit on the head with an axe?
A splitting headache.

What happened to Ray when he fell off the
  cliff?
He became X-Ray.

BOSS: Smith! Why are you late for work?
SMITH: I'm sorry, sir, but the house blew up.
  My parents were both killed, my sister
  was blinded, and my brother lost both
  his legs.
BOSS: Very well. I'll overlook it this time,
  but see that it doesn't happen again.

On a school outing a boy rushed up to a
teacher. 'Sir,' he panted, 'Harrington just
fell over the cliff!'
  'Is he hurt?' asked the teacher.
  'I don't know,' replied the boy. 'He was
still falling when I left.'

Why did Henry VIII have so many wives?
Because he liked to chop and change.

CYRIL: Why were you late on Thursday,
  Cecil?
CECIL: My car got a puncture.
CYRIL: Did you drive over a nail?
CECIL: No, over a bottle of lemonade.
CYRIL: But didn't you see it in the road?
CECIL: No, the silly child had it hidden
  under his jumper.

What's the result of smoking too much?
Coffin.

NELLIE: I was sorry to hear your head
  teacher died. What was the complaint?
SMELLIE: I don't think there have been any
  yet.

What's big, red, and lies upside-down in
  the gutter?
A dead bus.

Camilla dropped her baby brother out of
the window. She'd heard him described as
a bouncing baby and wanted to find out if it
was true.

'Dad, is it true that before we are born we
  are dust, and after we're dead we're dust
  too?'
'Yes, son.'
'Well, come quickly. There's someone
  under my bed and I don't know if he's
  coming or going.'

'Dad, are you sure it's true that we are
  made of dust?'
'Yes, son.'
'Then how come I don't get muddy when I
  go swimming?'

MRS STINK: When my husband saw the
   Grand Canyon his face dropped a mile.
MRS SINK: Was he disappointed?
MRS STINK: No, he fell over the edge.

Stinker and Pongo were walking through
the churchyard one night. The wind was
howling in the trees, blowing a few ragged
clouds across the moon. Stinker shivered.
   'What's up?' asked Pongo.
   'Listen,' said Stinker, his teeth
chattering.
   A voice came faintly from the direction of
a large family tomb, where someone had
been buried recently. 'First I'm going to eat
your head, then I'm going to eat your feet,
then I'm going to eat your arms . . .'
   'Blimey!' said Pongo. 'Let's get out of
here!'
   They ran for the exit, but before they
could get out of the gate a figure in black
loomed before them.
   'I thought I heard someone,' said the
vicar. 'Would you like a jelly baby, Stinker
and Pongo?'